MOTIVATION

Rob Long

David Fulton Publishers Ltd
The Chiswick Centre, 414 Chiswick High Road, London W4 5TF

www.fultonpublishers.co.uk

First published in Great Britain by David Fulton Publishers in association
with the National Association for Special Educational Needs (NASEN)

NASEN is a registered charity no. 1007023.

David Fulton Publishers is a division of Granada Learning Limited, part
of ITV plc.

British Library Cataloguing in Publication Data
A catalogue record for this book is available from the British Library.

ISBN 184312 365 7

Typeset by FiSH Books, London
Printed and bound in Great Britain

Contents

1 Introduction

Anyone working with young people has an interest in what motivates them. Why do children think, feel and behave as they do? Motivation is at the heart of teaching learners of all ages and abilities. With a clearer understanding of motivation in school we are better able to understand and support those young people who find learning at best a chore and at worst something to be actively fought against. Yet, while many students are quickly labelled as 'demotivated', they can seem incredibly motivated – not to be motivated.

There are many questions that, on the surface, seem baffling and confusing:

- Why will students work hard in one lesson but not in another?
- Why will a reward work one day but not the next?
- Why will students say they understand when they don't?
- Why won't students work when they could easily succeed?

One of the problems with understanding motivation is that the finger of blame is nearly always pointed immediately at the student. We have become so used to believing young people to be responsible for their behaviour that we tend to ignore the context they are in. We would all agree, however, that some lessons can be boring and that some tasks can be beyond the ability of a student. We need to look at motivation as something that is influenced by:

- the characteristics of the individual
- the context the individual is in.

The wider our understanding of motivation the more effective our interventions will be. Motivation is not difficult to understand, as this booklet will show. It will provide insight and understanding as well as diagnostic tools and interventions to support those children who, in certain situations, when faced with certain tasks, presented by certain people, lack motivation.

With motivation:

- goals and objectives are more easily achieved
- lessons are enjoyed
- absences are reduced
- teams and individuals function more harmoniously and effectively.

A motivated student is one who arrives on time to lessons, has the correct equipment and seeks appropriate support to ensure success.

Without motivation:

- effort and persistence are reduced
- increased support and supervision become essential
- conflict and disharmony increase
- absenteeism increases.

A lack of motivation can explain why some students make little effort to learn and fail to complete assignments that are within their ability. Such students do not participate in lessons nor do they ask for support when they fail to understand.

Some motivation myths

Myth 1 – students who do not try in school are unmotivated
False. Students who fear failure can be highly motivated to protect their self-esteem.

Myth 2 – achievement is greatest when the grades students achieve are awarded on a competitive basis
False. Students who have a history of failure will give up quickly as they expect not to succeed.

Myth 3 – the bigger the reward, the harder students will try
False. Without an expectation of success rewards fail to motivate.

Personal awareness

Often the best way to make sense of the factors that affect our students is to look within ourselves. As you work through the questions below think of how they might apply to a student you know. (Some possible answers are on p. 6)

Question 1 – think of one thing that you are quite good at
In a few words – how did you become good at it?

Question 2 – think of a personal quality that you feel good about
In a few words – how do you know you can feel good about it? What evidence do you have?

Question 3 – think of one thing that you are not good at
In a few words – what went wrong?

Question 4 – think of something that you did learn successfully, but which at the time you did not want to learn
In a few words – can you explain what kept you at it?

From a very personal and practical point of view we now have a range of key factors affecting motivation that apply not only to us but also to our students.

Successful learning depends on:

- *wanting* – the more a goal relates to a student's personal interests and emotional needs the higher will be his/her motivation
- *doing* – opportunities to practise a new skill or understanding are essential for good learning
- *feedback* – constructive, positive feedback maintains motivation
- *understanding* – the more a new skill or understanding is linked into a student's existing framework the deeper and more meaningful the learning experience will be.

A definition

Some important points seem already to be emerging. One of the key observations, however, is that students' motivation can vary across situations and from time to time. Our definition needs to reflect the changing nature of motivation.

> Motivation is a state of readiness or eagerness to change, which may fluctuate from one time or situation to another. This state is one that can be influenced.
>
> (Miller and Rollnick, 1991)

Tips for lesson planning

Any lesson can be motivating or demotivating. It is worth detailing those aspects of a lesson that can increase a student's level of arousal, that is his/her motivation to learn.

Beginning a lesson
- Do students know the lesson objectives?
- Is their curiosity aroused?
- Is the work linked to their personal needs and goals?
- Are they aware of the skills they will master?
- Is there a range of activities to be completed?
- Is there an element of fun and surprise?

During a lesson
- Are there opportunities for practice?
- Can students obtain support quickly and effectively?
- Do students work collaboratively?
- Am I using a range of teaching methods?
- Can all students achieve extrinsic rewards?

Ending a lesson
- Is there a constructive review of the lesson?
- Are students aware of how the new knowledge/skills fit with their existing ones?
- Do students receive feedback for effort, competency, participation and achievement?
- Have the students experienced success through increasing their control?

When students fail to engage with lessons there may well be good reasons:

- Is the work set at an appropriate level?
- Does the student have the necessary skills for success? (Listening, organisational, etc.)
- Are there any physical (visual) or medical reasons why they cannot learn successfully?
- Are you aware of any changes in a student's home circumstances that could be emotionally distracting?

The student's perspective
- Are you aware of the student's values, needs and expectations?
- Are the learning outcomes challenging and relevant to the learner?
- Does the learner have the necessary skills?
- Are there plenty of opportunities for practice and success?
- Are the targets meaningful?
- Have you involved the student in setting the learning targets?
- Are you giving regular feedback and encouragement?

Personal awareness exercise: possible answers (from p. 3)

Question 1
Practice, determination, feedback, encouragement, enthusiasm.

Question 2
Feedback, other people, friends.

Question 3
Lack of practice, criticism, no interest.

Question 4
Long-term goal, reward, to show people I could do it, to please others, to avoid punishment, overcoming a challenge.

2 The learning process and personality

There are, of course, many factors that affect how well students learn. A useful model to hold in mind is that of the learning stages that students, and we ourselves, go through (see Figure 1). This model has especial relevance for those older students who become disenchanted with subjects they find boring. They also find it hard to relate positively to those adults whose management style is confrontational. Adolescents are less inclined passively to accept being treated as 'children' but being expected to act like 'adults'.

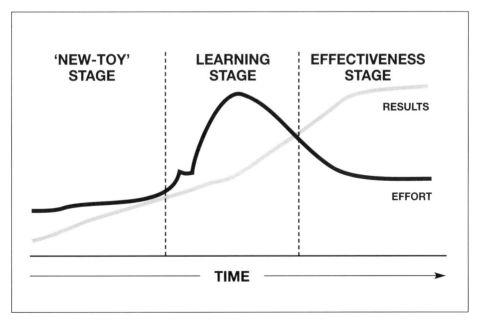

FIGURE 1. Learning stages

The motivational dip

It is common at the beginning of any enterprise, lesson, project, whatever, for there to be a high level of motivation/interest/arousal. *But* at the beginning of any learning there is a need for a lot of effort with very little payback as we try to master new skills or concepts. This scant return for maximum effort results in many students giving up. They experience what is known as the motivational dip (see Figure 2). (Who has not experienced this? It is normal.)

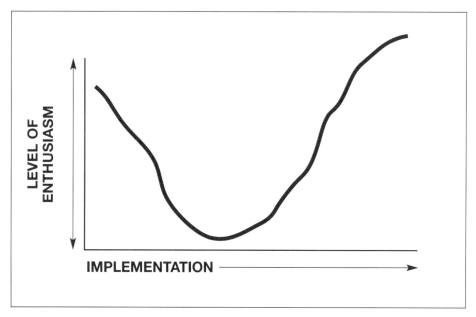

FIGURE 2. The motivational dip

However if effort can be maintained through the early stages of an activity there comes a point when reduced effort produces increased returns as we master the task. Our aim for learners who are at risk of giving up quickly is to break tasks down into small achievable steps and to make sure that they receive feedback on their progress. At this stage the feedback needs to be specific and forceful to maintain their motivation through the motivational dip.

Recognition and feedback

Rather than being given rewards the learners need to be reassured that their efforts are paying off. We need to accentuate the positive when giving feedback on each of their small steps towards total success. Record sheets should magnify the progress they are making.

Learning styles

Today we appreciate the different learning styles that students have. A well-known classification identifies three contrasting styles:

- visual
- auditory
- kinesthetic.

Individual learners prefer to receive new information in individual ways: either by seeing, hearing or feeling. While it is helpful to be aware of this, it is a rare lesson today where a teacher only uses one sense to input information to students. Most teachers tackle the differing ways in which students learn by using a range of methods in their lessons. For example a contemporary social topic is taught through showing Year 7 students video examples, letting them read actual accounts as well as interviewing participants of the events. Current topics could include investigating the need for skate parks or how young people's views are taken into account by local councils.

The best way to ensure that we vary our teaching methods is to remember the old Chinese adage:

> I hear and I forget.
> I see and I remember.
> I do and I understand.

Another useful classification focuses on the preferred manner by which students process information. There are four common styles:

- *reflective* – likes to think and observe
- *pragmatist* – enjoys seeing how practical problems can be solved
- *theorist* – enjoys new ideas and concepts
- *activist* – enjoys hands-on experience.

Using this latter classification it is possible to see how certain teaching methods are likely to engage certain learning styles more than others. Figure 3 shows the most preferred methods for each learning style. It may be used as an *aide mémoire* to ensure that a lesson has a wide range of methods so that each student's preferred learning style is at times being tapped.

Personality style

If we compared the personality attributes of most school staff with those students who face social, emotional and behavioural difficulties we would see a marked contrast. School staff would probably score high on such attributes as being determined, hard working and committed, while our sample of students would score higher on rebelliousness, daydreaming and attention-seeking. We are not always in the best position to understand the challenges they face, but being aware of our students' different attributes enables us to try to ensure that some of the teaching methods we use tap into relevant aspects of their personality. Figure 4 shows that the rebel will enjoy role play, group work and real-life practice, while the dreamer will prefer problem-solving, reflection and observational learning.

By designing our lessons with reference to both these models we can ensure that they will enable as many of our students as possible to feel actively involved, using teaching methods that match their preferred thinking and personality style.

METHOD	INFORMATION LEARNING STYLE			
	REFLECTIVE	PRAGMATIST	THEORIST	ACTIVE
ROLE PLAY				✓
REFLECTION	✓			
PROBLEM-SOLVING		✓		
GROUP WORK				
CASE STUDY		✓		
PRESENTATION			✓	
VIDEO	✓			
QUESTIONNAIRE			✓	
WORKPLACE PRACTICE				✓
QUIZ			✓	
OBSERVATIONAL LEARNING	✓			
PEER COACHING		✓		

FIGURE 3. Learning grid and methods

METHOD	PERSONAL STYLE		
	REBEL	DREAMER	ATTENTION SEEKER
ROLE PLAY	✓		
GROUP WORK	✓		
REAL LIFE PRACTICE	✓		
PEER COACHING			✓
1:1 SUPPORT			✓
SIMULATIONS			✓
PROBLEM-SOLVING		✓	
REFLECTION		✓	
OBSERVATIONAL LEARNING		✓	

FIGURE 4. Personal style and methods

The learning profile

All students develop their own preferred ways of learning. This is the result of interactions between the individual (biology and developmental personal characteristics) and his/her social world. Knowledge of a student's learning style can help the student and us to construct preferential learning experiences that will engage and motivate him/her. It can also serve as a useful framework through which a positive relationship can develop between the learner and the adult.

Help the student complete the assessment profile below.

Learning preferences assessment

1. Perceptual preference
Does the student prefer to listen, see or actively take part in new learning?

2. Learning style
What is the student's preferred learning style?
>   activist
>   theorist
>   pragmatist
>   reflector

3. Environmental factors
Does the student work better in the morning or afternoon? Does she or he prefer noise or quiet?
>   noise v. quiet
>   morning v. afternoon

4. Social factors
Can the student learn best alone or in the company of others?

3 The attribution process

Two core aspects of motivation are the student's self-worth and his or her attribution process. The attribution process is the way in which learners make sense to themselves of their behaviour. In other words, when learners fail, they might put it down to:

internal reasons
- they didn't revise enough
- they lack the necessary ability

external reasons
- they were poorly taught
- the questions were extremely hard – no one could do them.

Naturally the way they explain matters to themselves will affect their motivation in the future and their self-esteem. It is worth noting here that there is a general gender difference: girls tend to use more internal explanations when they fail – negative-prone failure attributions, while boys tend to use more external ones – they blame the teacher, the work, etc.

Student responses to failure

Why is it that two students who both fail a test respond so differently?

- Student A fails a test but becomes fired with increased determination to improve on the next one. The student knows that with more preparation he or she can make progress.
- Student B fails and becomes increasingly depressed. The student feels ashamed, and failure immobilises him or her, preventing preparation for the next test.

The difference between these students is the manner in which they explain their failure to themselves.

Attributional styles

Three common attributional styles that have been identified and studied are:

1. Learned helplessness
This is a lack of effort in specific situations. Through experiencing repeated failure learners come to believe that they are unable to succeed in certain tasks; that no matter how hard they try they will fail. Consequently they make little effort.

Such students respond to problems with a complete overreaction; failure seems to trigger a negative downhill spiral, a sense that they will never be able to improve, and results in such outcomes as 'maths phobia'.

2. Fear of failure
Learners who are prepared to attempt difficult tasks tend to attribute failure to internal causes, for example lack of effort. This means they are aware that they have some control and can therefore improve through effort. However, those learners who fear failure have a weaker self-esteem. They see failure as being caused by factors beyond their control and believe there is nothing they can do to improve their results. Fear of failure is an emotionally controlled way of protecting a learner's fragile self-esteem.

3. Lack of ability
Some learners are convinced that they lack ability and that no amount of effort can change this. When they do succeed they often attribute success to luck or easy challenges. 'Lack of ability' is the student's cognitive explanation for his or her failure.

By asking the right questions of the learner we can ascertain the type of attribution process she or he is employing in a particular situation.

The right questions will also tap into three core aspects of the attribution process:

1. *Locus of control*
Does the student believe the reasons for failure are within his or her control (internal), or not (external)?

2. *Stability*
Is the student's success or failure a short-term occurrence or predictive of future outcomes?

3. *Control*
Does the student believe she or he can change matters or not?

Through circling the answers a student gives in Table 1 it is possible to see whether it is faulty attributions that are contributing to a student's lack of motivation.

Attribution training

It is understandable that attribution processes that have been learned over time are not going to be quickly changed. If learners have formed the mind-set that when they fail it is because of their lack of ability or the teacher's poor instruction, for example, a major change of perspective is required for them to believe that with more effort they could do better. It is comparable to turning the naturally pessimistic person into an optimist. It can be done – but it takes time. There are a number of techniques that can be used to help develop the learner's belief in his or her own power to overcome difficulties and the assurance that success is not impossible.

Effort training
Teach learners to recognise when their failure is due to low effort and reward them when they acknowledge this. For example, ask the student to gauge on an effort scale how much effort they think a particular task

DIMENSIONS	ATTRIBUTIONS	
	TEST SUCCESS POSITIVE	TEST FAILURE NEGATIVE
	LOCUS OF CONTROL	
INTERNAL V EXTERNAL	I WORKED HARD I WAS LUCKY	I DIDN'T REVISE BAD LUCK
	STABILITY	
STABLE V UNSTABLE	I'M GOOD AT TESTS I WORKED ON THE RIGHT TOPICS	I GET STRESSED IT WAS A HARD TEST
	CONTROLLABILITY	
CONTROLLABLE V UNCONTROLLABLE	I PLANNED AND REVISED SOMEBODY UP THERE LIKES ME	I REVISED OTHER SUBJECTS TOO MUCH WHY DOES EVERYTHING ALWAYS GO WRONG

TABLE 1. The attribution process

is going to take: 'So, Jack, to complete this page of maths problems how much effort do you think it will need? Remember that yesterday the page you thought would require little effort, I think you gave it a 2 rating, was not as easy as you expected.'

Effort scale

Little		Moderate		A lot
1	2	3	4	5

Success training

Set realistically obtainable goals. For example, 'OK, Shakeela, you are going to write a short story about your holiday. Let's look at what will be your first steps then we can build it from there. You were telling me about the people you were going to include. That sounds like a good place to start. Make a list of who is going to be in the story, and then describe them.' When learners succeed at their goals, support them in attributing their success to the effort they put in.

Cognitive dissonance

This is when two thoughts conflict with each other. Thinking negatively about sport and then volunteering to join a team activity produces a tension that needs to be resolved. In adults a common example would be 'I know I smoke', but, conversely, 'I also like to keep healthy'. With encouragement and advice on how to tackle areas of particular difficulty learners can be helped to succeed. The adult can then highlight the discrepancy in their thinking: 'You said you couldn't do that problem. But look you have. You'll have to tell yourself you can do those problems from now on.'

Challenging

With a supportive adult the learner can examine some of his or her faulty beliefs against the evidence he or she is using. For example, 'You're saying you've had a really bad term. Let's have a look at your results because I am not sure they are as bad as you think.'

Reframing

The learner can be helped to explore a number of alternative explanations for his or her behaviour. For example, 'You are disappointed at your homework mark, but let's look at the pressures you have been coping with lately. You have just moved into a new house and you told me last week that your Gran was in hospital. Do you think these worries might explain why you have not been so focused on your work and why your mark was lower than usual?'

Self-reinforcement

The learner records and monitors his/her own behaviour over a period of time with agreed rewards for achieving set targets. For example, a student who leaves his or her seat for no sensible reason could record every time he or she does so. If the number is below a set target (perhaps six times in a lesson) the student can be allowed an agreed reward, such as extra computer time, to choose the class story book, etc.

4 Assessment tools and interventions

The causes behind an individual learner's behaviour comprise many interlocking factors, some of which are difficult to understand, and we may never have a complete picture of the complex set of influences in each student's life. Any attempt to explain behaviour is always, in any event, a gross simplification. Some of the factors to consider are:

- biological factors – such as an inherited disposition to be tall or short
- genetic factors – such as dyslexia
- developmental phase – what level of emotional self-control they have achieved
- family – for example, parenting style (authoritarian, authoritative, democratic)
- attitude – for example, 'you have no right to make me work at home'
- personality/temperament – are they calm or prone to anxiety?
- attributions – do they quickly blame others or accept responsibility for their own behaviour?
- school experiences – do they feel safe and part of their group?
- etc., etc.

But we are not looking for definitive explanations. We are looking for clues that help us understand the reason for a learner's behaviour in a particular context. This is much easier and more relevant to us when we are seeking appropriate interventions. Drawing on theoretical explanations as well as applied research we will look at two practical approaches to help us understand and support those students who do not engage with our lessons.

The first we will call *a functional analysis of behaviour*. This allows us to understand the 'why' of our students' behaviour through looking at what it achieves for them. Kate, for example, is frequently out of her seat and disrupting other students. As a result her teacher has to keep reprimanding her. A functional analysis of behaviour will ask what Kate's behaviour is 'earning' for her. It seems that there are several related needs being met:

- Kate is avoiding work
- Kate is receiving both peer and adult attention.

By understanding the function of her behaviour we can use interventions that will help Kate satisfy some of her needs in a less disruptive manner.

The second approach considers what we will call *motivational barriers*. By this I mean those commonly understood reasons why some students seem to lack motivation to work (see list of motivational barriers on pp. 22 and 25).

Many of the problems that demotivate and prevent students from engaging with the work they are set stem from what are known as *mistaken goals*:

- *habitual* – an over-learned pattern of behaviour that occurs automatically in specific situations – as seen in the student who argues whenever confronted with learning challenges
- *attention* – the need for attention, even if it involves negative feedback – from the student who seeks reassurance and approval after each small step is completed. In a Year 2 group, for example, Randeep is painting a picture of his house and garden. Every time he draws in a small part he leaves his seat to ask his teacher, 'Is this all right?' In 15 minutes he has left his seat eight times
- *power* – the need to have control in situations by challenging any reprimand and being prepared to increase the conflict
- *revenge* – the need to cause pain and hurt as a release to personal pain – demonstrated by the student who secretly spoils another child's painting, for example

- *nurture* – the need to have an adult who will care and parent them as, for example, when a student is unable to attempt work unless supported by an adult one-to-one
- *escape* – the need to avoid work that could lead to failure – shown by the student who engages in avoidance activities such as sharpening pencils.

Whether it is these mistaken goals that are driving a student's behaviour in class can be discerned through asking good questions. Because behaviour is functional, that is it seeks to obtain a certain outcome, we can often infer the mistaken goal that is driving the behaviour by looking at what it achieves for a student. Figure 5 presents a range of indicative questions that will enable us to hypothesise which are the strongest influences behind a set behaviour. It is not uncommon for behaviour to be driven by several factors – young people are as complicated as you or me.

Now that we have one or two hypotheses we can choose some interventions that we can use to help the learners satisfy their internal needs in ways that are more appropriate within the school and classroom context (see Figure 6).

Motivational barriers

Failure syndrome. Some students are so used to failing that they no longer make much effort. If you expect to fail, what is the point of expending excessive energy? These students are often able but have had negative learning experiences that have lowered their expectations.

Disaffection. It is not uncommon for some students, especially during the adolescent years, to become disaffected. This is a shorthand way both of saying they see little relevance to them of the curriculum they are expected to study and also of challenging the rights of adults to control them now that they are 'adults' themselves.

HABITUAL

Does the behaviour:

1. Happen mainly when the student is on his/her own or bored? **Y   N**
2. Make the student unaware of his/her surroundings? **Y   N**
3. Stop when the student is distracted? **Y   N**
4. Have a set pattern/set of actions? **Y   N**
5. Persist despite requests to stop? **Y   N**

SCORE_____

ATTENTION

Does the behaviour:

1. Stop when attention is given? **Y   N**
2. Only happen when the student has an audience? **Y   N**
3. Start up when attention is withdrawn? **Y   N**
4. Lead to negative feedback? **Y   N**
5. Make you feel annoyed or irritated? **Y   N**

SCORE_____

REVENGE

Does the behaviour:

1. Take place in private? **Y   N**
2. Persist despite sanctions? **Y   N**
3. Seem to be aimed at one person? **Y   N**
4. Hurt either themselves or others? **Y   N**
5. Make you feel sad and despairing? **Y   N**

SCORE_____

POWER

Does the behaviour:

1. Happen repeatedly? **Y   N**
2. Lead to a confrontational response? **Y   N**
3. Make you feel angry or frightened? **Y   N**
4. Gain control for the student? **Y   N**
5. Escalate when confronted? **Y   N**

SCORE_____

NURTURE

Does the behaviour:

1. Make you feel sympathetic and caring? **Y   N**
2. Result in the student being cared for? **Y   N**
3. Start up again when support is withdrawn? **Y   N**
4. Seem aimed at the same person? **Y   N**
5. Only happen in social situations? **Y   N**

SCORE_____

ESCAPE

Does the behaviour:

1. Happen in response to work being set? **Y   N**
2. Stop when appropriate work is given? **Y   N**
3. Result in the student being withdrawn? **Y   N**
4. Take place in different lessons? **Y   N**
5. Take place with different adults? **Y   N**

SCORE_____

STUDENT'S NAME_____   COMPLETED BY_____

DATE_____

FIGURE 5. Motivational assessment – a functional approach

23

HABITUAL	ATTENTION-SEEKING
1 Have distraction activities	1 Reward appropriate behaviour
2 Teach substitute activity	2 Catch them attending positively
3 Reward timed sessions without behaviour	3 Tactically ignore
4 Use non-verbal signal to stop behaviour	4 Arrange regular 1:1 contact
5 Encourage small signs of improvement	5 Sit with peer who models appropriate behaviour
6 Teach relaxation skills	6 Use 'pay back' system for time wasted
7 Reward incompatible behaviour	7 Teach appropriate behaviour

REVENGE	POWER
1 Build self-esteem	1 Give responsibilities, school council
2 Develop circle of friends	2 Side-step confrontations
3 Make life map of successes	3 Let them mentor a peer
4 Explore feelings through creative mediums and Art Therapy	4 Agree 'response plan' when confrontations develop
5 Agree 'reparation' activities	5 Let them lead an activity
6 Agree safety boundaries	6 Teach self-control
7 Develop empathy for others	7 Give them choices

MURTURE	ESCAPE
1 Reward 'I can' statements	1 Differentiate curriculum
2 Give safe choices	2 Provide sensitive support
3 Strengthen and develop social skills	3 Agree small targets
4 Teach positive self-statements	4 Teach new skills
5 Highlight existing skills	5 Reward requests for support
6 Review challenges faced and overcome	6 Use rewards for effort as well as achievements
7 Teach problem-solving skills	7 Use peer support

FIGURE 6. Motivational assessment – interventions

Underachievers. These students have a negative set of attitudes towards learning. They set unrealistic goals and yet tend to be too impulsive to persevere with assignments. These students often have the skills that would allow them to achieve, but see success as being dependent on factors outside of their control.

Boredom. These students tend to disrupt and distract others from their work. They convey an attitude of apathy and pointlessness towards any new activities. When they do work they expect rewards for the slightest effort they make.

Clearly, while these are listed as discrete motivational barriers, in reality most students will be affected by a mixture of several. An understanding of these different barriers does, however, allow us to become clearer as to the best interventions to put in place to support students who lack motivation (see Figures 5 and 6).

When we have produced a profile of some of the motivational barriers that a student is facing we can choose interventions most likely to prove effective from the intervention tool box.

Intervention tool box

Failure syndrome
- show faith and have positive expectations
- involve student in recording successes
- find a brilliant corner and harness it
- personalised differentiation – relate to learners' interests
- celebrate non-academic achievements
- make practice safe
- teach positive attributions for success

Disaffection
- build a relationship with the student
- let student set his/her own targets

- identify a role model
- arrange support for 'out of school' problems
- change the curriculum
- find a personal mentor they really like
- reward basics, e.g. attendance, punctuality, following rules

Underachievement
- differentiate and extend
- use alternative ways of learning
- get student to help someone less able
- explore reasons
- create a hierarchy of rewards
- encourage peer support
- set interesting homework and tasks

Boredom
- vary learning and teaching style
- make activities more exciting
- use games for learning
- give interactive/lively input
- encourage lively activity
- use music
- introduce sudden change of activity
- use discovery learning

5 The hard to reach

There will be a few children on whom the previous interventions will make little impact. These students are often described as being both reluctant and resistant learners. It is worth noting some of the negative factors that are probably holding a student in this state of affairs:

- a history of school failure
- negative adult feedback
- negative attitude
- poor organisational skills
- confrontational defence style
- real or imagined peer approval

... the list goes on.

Student resistance

Our efforts to help students who are firmly trapped in an anti-learning attitude will typically meet with resistance. The harder we push the harder they push back – this response is in itself a normal psychological reaction. Such students are naturally reluctant to step into the unknown by responding differently to challenges than in the negative way that they have learned over a long period of time. They are unlikely to change their responses just because you or I ask them to.

It is important to remember that, while we are attempting to change students' behaviour through positive interventions, there remain many negative factors in their life which support their existing behaviour. If ours were the only influences on them life would be so much easier! From the students' point of view their behaviour remains functional in fulfilling their needs and/or defending them from challenges that are beyond them.

Building a relationship with the student

It is relationships that give our lives meaning. Just think for a moment of the difference between an *interaction* and a *relationship*. Interactions are usually short in duration, functional and unemotional, while a relationship lasts for some time, is emotional and enjoyable.

Our approach in trying to reach such 'hard to reach' students is to create an open, honest and trusting relationship with the student. When we have that a student may begin openly to consider the advantages of change. Without such a relationship we are in danger of just being another 'well-meaning adult' trying to change them – and the student is understandably defensive. (Resistance to changing well-established patterns of behaviour is not abnormal – it is normal. All of us relapse when we try to break ingrained habits.)

Students with SEBD

Students with social, emotional and behavioural difficulties are at high risk of experiencing motivational difficulties. This is because their difficulties will usually have been barriers to them engaging with learning experiences. As a result they will tend to have had more negative experiences in school through reprimands and punishments and their attitude towards learning is not surprisingly negative, reflecting an apparent lack of motivation. In the learning situation they are likely to experience anxiety and insecurity.

The ways in which students react to such distress are likely to fall under two headings:

- *active defensiveness* – the student 'assaults' the authority figure by means of disruptive behaviour

- *passive withdrawal* – the student withdraws from the situation and will not contribute or respond when questioned. The student's fear of failure pushes him/her into a protective shell. Such students can easily be overlooked in a lesson because they present little active challenge.

These responses are more commonly known as 'fight or flight'. The challenge for any adult working with such students is to enable them to experience success as well as a sense of hope that matters can improve through a secure and trusting relationship. The adult serves then as a mediator between the student as learner and the task to be learned.

Note. The relationship we need to build with our students is, of course, a professional one – we are not looking to become their best friend and we need at all times to make this clear. If we are working with adolescents they can easily, and sometimes wilfully, misread our attempt to build a supportive relationship with them. If a relationship begins to make you feel uneasy, be guided by your emotions. Discuss the matter with colleagues. Try to work with the student only in small groups or when there are other adults present. Do not let matters get out of hand.

Relationship-building skills

General strategies

- spend time with the student
- disclose appropriate self-information, such as personal hobbies, football team supported, musical interests
- show high expectations
- develop rituals and traditions, for example play a special piece of music whenever a learner does something outstanding
- link with their friends and home.

Specific techniques

When you have built a positive relationship with the student you will be able to discuss and work with him or her to find ways to improve his or her motivation.

Cost–benefit analysis

Try to be clear as to the benefits students will obtain by improving their commitment to work. What are the advantages and disadvantages? Do they have a long-term goal? Does effort now play a part in achieving it? Help students to understand that it is not just 'the piece of paper' that they will achieve. They will learn a wide range of life skills:

- to work as a team member
- to be a leader
- to communicate
- to problem-solve
- to manage confrontations
- negotiation skills.

Norm of reciprocity

There is a fundamental norm at work in all relationships – it is known as the 'norm of reciprocity'. In English that means 'you scratch my back and I'll scratch yours'. If someone helps you or does you a good turn, then there is a degree of expectation/obligation that if they ask you for help you will help them. When possible the more help/support you offer students the more likely they are to help you when you ask. Offering to lend them books or equipment are all ways of investing in the 'emotional bank'.

Locus of control

Many students have experienced little age-appropriate autonomy and have little control in their lives. Refusing to work can be an attempt to gain some control. This will be especially true during adolescence – a time when they are expected to take more control over their lives. Some adolescents will express their need for control by refusing to be helped by adults. Make every effort to allow them to set their own learning targets.

With the more difficult to reach students some of the following interventions may be used in conjunction with a good relationship:

Wagering
Students often like a challenge: 'I'll make you a coffee if you can complete this questionnaire in 10 minutes.'

Law of effect
Explaining what is in it for the young person if they make an effort to learn can help them to see what is to be gained or lost.

Personal notes
When a young person finds it difficult to talk, write them a note saying, for example, that you are glad they came and hope that they will talk when they are ready to.

Teaching strategic skills
Agree to help the young person achieve a specific goal and work with him or her to develop skills to achieve the goal.

Termination as motivation
'I understand that you don't want to have six sessions with me. How about it if we work hard and reduce that to three sessions.'

Cost–benefit analysis
Work out with students the gains to them of keeping with their present behaviour and the losses, and the gains and losses if they change.

Emotional change technique
Teach young people that by thinking of certain memories they can learn to change what they are feeling. For example, if they have an especially happy holiday memory, or a funny incident that happened in school, help them to use the memory to re-experience the feeling that they had. With practice they can change their mood by focusing on the memory and the feelings that went with it.

Scaling technique
On a scale of 1 to 10, with 1 being the worst this problem has ever been

and 10 the best, where would you rate things today? What is going well? What are you doing? What is the next thing you need to do to improve things by 1 or 2 points.

Miracle question

Imagine tonight while you are asleep a miracle happens and this problem is solved. How will you be able to tell the next day that a miracle has happened? No matter how small it is, start tomorrow 'as if' the miracle has happened.

Problem-free talk

Ask the student to speak for a minute about a hobby/interest he or she has. Use this to build a relationship as well as noting his/her skills and personal qualities.

The Columbo technique

Practise 'strategic incompetence'. Ask the student, 'Have you any ideas as to what might help?'

6 Motivational Equity

Too often the students we are trying to involve in learning are in contexts where rewards are determined by achievements. Given that many of these students would define themselves as lacking the ability to achieve, is it any wonder that they make little effort to obtain the rewards?

Motivational Equity (ME) means that *all* have an equal chance of obtaining rewards because the rewards are linked to learning and effort rather than ability and achievement. This is totally in keeping with an inclusive philosophy. Many students with SEBD, for example, are in fact discriminated against because their disability means that they cannot compete on a 'level playing field' with their peers. However ME allows everyone to achieve, irrespective of ability, background or disability.

In classrooms where ME is practised there is not less learning, there is more. The following principles can be used in a classroom, small group or in a one-to-one situation.

ME principles

The work set is always challenging but within the reach of the student. Tasks are made interesting and linked to real life, with the aim of making them as relevant to the individual student as is possible. The problems presented are intended to tap into a learner's curiosity as well as his or her desire to master new skills.

ME has helped to motivate Vimla, for example, who was finding her geography work less than interesting. Her teacher has devised a project for her around one of her key interests – lions. Now Vimla is learning about the places where lions live and how different countries are trying to protect them.

ME is also helping to improve Tim's negative attitude towards his ball skills, which has stopped him from joining in with his friends when football is played at break times. His support assistant has worked out with Tim a number of activities that are improving his hand–eye coordination. Tim is being helped to record his progress and is beginning to see that he can catch and throw better through regular practice. The next step is for him to play ball games with just a few friends.

Recognition is obtained as a result of the effort learners bring to their tasks as well as their originality in posing new questions and creating new solutions. The ways in which recognition is given will vary, but praise, merit points, certificates, choice of activities and so on will be used. The key point is that there are more than enough rewards for all – there is no scarcity or limit on them.

All students come to see that if they participate and make progress they will be recognised/rewarded. There is no discrimination against those who face a range of disabilities which can limit their learning potential if compared to others – they should be compared against themselves. This also benefits able learners. When there are set rewards for set achievements students who can achieve tend only to do as much as is necessary to earn the reward. ME encourages all students to find and fulfil their own learning potential.

Self-belief is developed through emphasising, modelling and reinforcing learners' personal control. Students are encouraged to challenge inappropriate self-beliefs that focus on ability and achievement. In the ME class ability is seen more as a process than a fixed entity; it is the capacity to modify and develop the student's repertoire of skills; it is fluid and dynamic, rather than fixed and static.

Personal responsibility

Failure is often caused by students setting unrealistic goals: either too hard or too easy. By offering support and developing their confidence,

ME helps students to set realistic targets and aim for achievements that are within their competency range. This immediately increases the chance of success and reinforces new beliefs within the student. Nothing breeds success like success. For many students we need to help them overcome their learned fear of success as much as their learned fear of failure.

A case study

At 10 years old, Martin, who has learning difficulties, was causing serious concern to his teacher. His school records showed his behaviour deteriorating as the school year progressed. In class he seemed to be constantly on the move, rarely completing any piece of work without some form of reprimand from his teacher. His impulsiveness meant that he acted without thinking, which resulted in him interfering with other pupils who were working.

Investigations suggested that Martin has few good role models at home, and he has been spotted in the local town mixing with older children who have a history of truanting.

When interviewed about his behaviour and poor attitude towards learning Martin displayed mixed feelings. He seemed to want to do better but said that he found the work either too hard or just boring.

Interventions
His class teacher took a multifaceted approach and employed the following ME strategies:

- Through exploring Martin's interests work was set in the following areas to draw on his natural curiosity:
  - reptiles – Martin had a pet terrapin
  - art – Martin was a good drawer, especially of cartoon characters.
- A positive self-belief was encouraged through Martin producing a photo collage of his work for display in the reception area.
- He also kept a diary, with the help of a support assistant, of the

targets he set himself each day and how he solved any difficulties in meeting those targets.

- In class Martin was given a small number of activities – read a book, tidy up the play area, etc. – to do whenever he felt he needed a rest from the work he was doing.
- At all times school staff focused on those times when Martin was engaged with learning and behaving appropriately, for which there was a range of positive consequences. A points system had been devised, with Martin, which enabled him to choose from a menu of rewards. These ranged from low-level rewards, such as choosing who he could sit with, to *Winner* certificates to take home.

Outcome

At first progress was slow. Martin seemed to find all the increased attention difficult to cope with. However with caring persistence his work output increased and his in-class behaviour improved. While difficult days did occur they were gradually becoming fewer. When last interviewed Martin spoke about the increased number of rewards he was receiving and how he felt he was getting on better with his classmates.

And finally

There will of course be those who will say that this degree of flexibility to meet the needs of one pupil is unfair. What about the attention and time that is being taken away from the other pupils? But surely if we treated all pupils as if they were the same then that would be unfair. Some pupils need individual programmes such as Martin's to motivate them to succeed. Being fair is about enabling all children to be included and achieve their potential. Martin was not getting more than he needed, he was getting what he needed. Other children at other times have different needs.

Further reading

Reference

Miller, R. and Rollnick, S. (1991) *Motivational interviewing*. New York: The Guilford Press.

Recommended reading

Brophy, J. (1998) *Motivating students to learn*. New York: McGraw-Hill.

Burden, P. R. (2000) *Powerful classroom management strategies: motivating students to learn*. Thousand Oaks, California: Corwin Press Inc.

Dreikurs, R., Grunwald, B. and Pepper, F. (1998) *Maintaining sanity in the classroom: classroom management techniques*. London: Accelerated Development.

Galloway, D., Rogers, C., Armstrong, D. and Leo, E. (1998) *Motivating the difficult to reach*. London: Longman.

McNamara, E. (1998) *Motivational interviewing*. Positive Behaviour Management. Available from: 7 Quinton Close, Ainsdale, Merseyside PR8 2TD.

Pintrich, P. and Schunk, D. (1996) *Motivation in education*. Englewood Cliffs, New Jersey: Prentice Hall.

Riding, R. and Rayner, S. (1998) *Cognitive styles & learning strategies*. London: David Fulton.

Selekman, M. (1993) *Pathways to change*. New York: The Guilford Press.

Sommers-Flanagan, J. and Sommers-Flanagan, R. (1997) *Tough kids cool counselling*. Alexandria, USA: American Counseling Association.

The complete set of titles in Rob Long's Building Success Through Better Behaviour series:

The Art of Positive Communication: A practitioner's guide to managing behaviour
1 84312 367 3

Better Behaviour
1 84312 363 0

Children's Thoughts and Feelings
1 84312 368 1

Loss and Separation
1 84312 364 9

Motivation
1 84312 365 7

Obsessive Compulsive Disorders
1 84312 366 5

Working with Groups
1 84312 371 1

Yeah Right! Adolescents in the classroom
1 84312 370 3

David Fulton Publishers

NASEN

Special Needs and Drug Education	1-84312-360-6	£12.00
Supporting Mathematical Thinking	1-84312-362-2	£18.00
Dyslexia and Inclusion	1-84312-361-4	£17.00

To order these books please contact:
David Fulton Publishers Ltd
The Chiswick Centre • 414 Chiswick High Road • London W4 5TF
Tel: 020 8996 3610 • Fax: 020 8996 3622
www.fultonpublishers.co.uk